Soul Words

Michelle Sierens

◆ FriesenPress

Suite 300 - 990 Fort St
Victoria, BC, V8V 3K2
Canada

www.friesenpress.com

ISBN
978-1-5255-1482-1 (Hardcover)
978-1-5255-1483-8 (Paperback)
978-1-5255-1484-5 (eBook)

1. SELF-HELP, PERSONAL GROWTH

Distributed to the trade by The Ingram Book Company

Dedicated To:

My Beautiful Grandchildren

Emma, Lila, Lauren,
Reid, Ethan, Andrew
Lane, Maylee & Abigail

Always Love and
Believe in Yourselves

No matter
Who You Are,
What You Do,
Where You Go
Grammie Will Always Love You

*"Our grandchildren are the bright flowers
in our garden of life."*

365 Daily Inspirational Word Phrases & Quotes

Simply
Opening
Up
Lovingly

Writing
Outstanding
Reflective
Descriptions
Simultaneously

My Incredible Spiritual Journey

Introduction

Welcome to my divine writings. Several years ago, I read the book *Writing the Divine,* by Sara Wiseman (Llewellyn Publications). She captured my curiosity, which led me to experiment with this style of writing. Without any knowledge of acrostic poetry, I dissected the word "beautiful," which led to the book you are about to read. It is simple yet deep and interesting yet powerful.

I have accumulated enough words to last an entire year. Reading one each day allows the reader time to contemplate the words that are written. I've included some words more than once, giving the reader an opportunity to think of the word in a different way. As my best friend said, "Your soul words totally need to be reread in order to gain greater meaning."

Therefore, thank you for taking the time to read and hopefully reread these words. May you be inspired to find your own definitions for these words. A table of contents has been included at the end of the book to make finding your favorite words quick and convenient.

Soul Words is yours to enjoy and share, to shelve, to gift, or just to pick up on a random day. My hope is simply that it inspires positive thoughts and actions.

May you enjoy this book as much as I have enjoyed writing it.

Love and Blessings,
Michelle Sierens

Beautiful

Being
Energizes
Aura,
Ultimately
Tapping
In,
Freeing
Ultra
Light

We are **beautiful**!

$\mathscr{T}$houghtful

Through

Helping

Others

Undeniably

Granting

Humans

Total

Fair

Utter

Love

Be **thoughtful!**

*W*isdom

What
Ignites
Soul
Deepens
Our
Minds

Wisdom is profound and gentle.

Care

Compassion
Always
Reaction
Eluded

Care about yourself.

Can

Capability

Apparent

Now

We **can** do anything, but the desire must be real.

Tender

Touching
Effortlessly,
Never
Doubting,
Endless
Reasons

Take a **tender** approach to life.

Smile

Seemingly
Momentarily
Illustrating
Love
Enlightened

A **smile** can change someone's day.

God

Great

Orchestra

Director

Thank you, **God,** for a new day and another opportunity to be the best that I can be.

Faith

Forever

Alleluia

In

The

Heart

Have **faith** in yourself.

Spirit

Sensing
Presence
Inward
Revering
In
Time

The **spirit** to share, to love, and to understand is within us all!

Calm

Catching
All
Little
Moments

Stay **calm** even when it storms.

Sunshine

Spraying

Uniformly

Natures

Sheer

Heat

Into

Numerous

Entities

Let the **sunshine** brighten your day.

$\mathcal{L}$aughter

Living

Aloud

Utter

Gut

Humor

To

Endless

Rhythms

Laughter is the music of the soul!

Glowing

Grounded

Luminance

Of

Women

In

Natal

Growth

A **glowing** ember flickers within
each and every one!

Creative

Consciously

Revealing

Excellent

Artistic

Talent

In

Various

Expressions

Be **creative;** it opens up a whole new world.

Fearless

Focusing

Energy

Ability,

Relaxing,

Laughing,

Enjoying,

Satisfying

Self

Be **fearless**!

Unique

Upon
Natural
Impression
Quiet
Unencumbered
Expression

We are **unique**!

Perfection

Precisely
Executing
Role,
Finding
Exact
Combination
To
Introducing
One's
Nature

Help another be aware of the **perfection**
that naturally lies within them.

$\mathscr{A}$wesome

Apparent
Wisdom
Exceeds,
Signaling
Outer
Magnificent
Energy

We are **awesome**!

Healthy

Having
Every
Alternative
Liking
The
Happy
You

Live **healthy**.

ℒove

Living
Open
Vulnerable
Evermore

Loving ourselves creates **love**
within for another.

Compassionate

Caring

Opens

Minds,

Pleasing

All

Senses,

Simply

Inspiring

Others,

Natural

Affection

Towards

Everyone

Be **compassionate!**

Wild

Wonderfully

Illustrating

Life's

Design

Show your **wild** side!

𝒻riendship

Finding
Real
Interesting
Energy,
Not
Demanding
Something,
Happiness
In
Progress

Friendship opens the door to get to know Self.

Enthusiasm

Enjoying

Naturally

The

Hype

U

See

In

A

Single

Moment

Enthusiasm is contagious.

Allow

Always
Loving
Letting
Others
Win

Allow others to travel their destined path.

$\mathcal{N}$onjudgmental

Not

Only

Not

Judging

U

Deciding

Goodness

Must

Emit

Naturally

To

All

Life

To be **nonjudgmental** is a wonderful choice.

Believe

Being

Effortlessly

Linked

Into

Everything

Versus

Evil

Believe in love!

*L*ove

Liking
Openly
Voiding
End

Love is a link to happiness.

Willingness

With
Initiative
Letting
Life
Inspire
Natural
Grace
Not
Expecting
Self
Standards

Be **willing**, be open, be fair, and be honest.

Spiritual

Sensing

Positive

Inspiration

Realizing

It

Totally

Unites

All

Life

Connect to your **spiritual** side and see life through a new set of eyes.

Free

Forever
Ready
Enjoying
Everything

We are **free** to be who we want to be!

Special

Something
Pretty
Exquisitely
Conveyed
Is
Attracting
Love

Do something **special** for your neighbor.

Good

Granting
Others
Opportunity
Daily

Be **good**!

Powerful

Providing

Others

With

Encouragement

Really

Feels

Utterly

Lovely

We are **powerful**!

*D*ependable

Disciplined

Energetic

Personality

Ensuring

No

Doubt,

Again

Beyond

Loyal

Evermore

Being **dependable** is to follow through with promises made to others and to Self!

Alert

Always
Listening
Early
Reaction
Time

Stay **alert**.

Bright

Beyond

Really

Interesting,

Great

Human

Talent

Children are a **bright** light in our lives.

ℒure

Love
Ultimately
Reels
Excitement

Extend your love and **lure** them in.

Power

Preying

Over

With

Eventual

Regret

Let the **power** struggle cease.

Bold

Boisterous

Open

Living

Defined

Bold & beautiful!

Rare

Realizing

A

Richness

Exists

Are we the **rare** gems or the common stones?

Fantastic

Fun

Acquiring

Nothing

Touchable

As

Seeing

The

Infant

Cackle

Life is **fantastic**!

Positive

Pleasing

Others

Signals

Inner

Thanks,

Inner

Voice

Excites

A **positive** outlook helps the flow of life.

Dance

Display
A
New
Creative
Existence

Let's dance our own dance.

Wonderful

Wicked

Ongoing

Natural

Displays

Expose

Real

Fulfilling

Ultra

Lessons

Always believe something **wonderful**
is about to happen.

Fair

Finding

Awareness

In

Respect

Fair should be the first unwritten rule.

Honest

Honor
Ones
Nature
Every
Single
Time

Being **honest** goes hand in hand
with being fair.

Generous

Giving

Eagerly,

Never

Ever

Rattled,

Open-handed

Unselfish

Simultaneously

Be **generous** indeed!

Charming

Charisma
Held
Allures,
Reaching
Many,
Inviting
Natural
Grace

Be kind and **charming**.

Fine

First

In

Natural

Excellence

Believe everything will be **fine**.

Delicate

Delightfully

Exquisite,

Letting

Innocence

Churn,

Arousing

Tender

Elegance

Don't trample a **delicate** flower.

$\mathcal{K}$ind

Knowledge

Is

Never

Disrespecting

Be **kind**!

Sensible

Sound
Example,
Noticeably
Shrewd,
Intelligently
Based
Logic
Expression

Living a **sensible** life keeps you from drowning.

Conform

Constant
Obeying,
Never
Fueling
Opportunities
Rendering
Magic

Conformity is the jailer of freedom
and the enemy of growth.

Judgment

Just
Understand,
Disrespect
Guarantees
Mental
Emotional
Never-ending
Torment

In judging another, **judgment** becomes
your thing.

Bad

Beyond
Acceptable
Decision

Bad is afraid of good.

Likable

Light
Ignites
Knowing
All
Brothers,
Linked
Energy

Don't waste time being **likable**,
just be yourself.

Reliable

Realizing

Effort

Leaves

Impression

After

Being

Loyal

Endlessly

To be **reliable** is to honor Self.

Lucky

Living
Unharmed
Charmed
Killer
Years

Make your own **lucky**!

Hot

Having
Obvious
Talent

Strike while the iron is **hot**!

Well

With
Every
Life
Luxury

Living **well** is a gift to Self.

Able

Attitude
Believes
Life
Energizes

We are **able** to see the light
despite the darkness.

Light

Luminescent
Images
Gradually
Hue
Together

Be the **light** in your family's life!

Shine

Sending
Hope
Irradiating
Naturally
Everywhere

Hold peace in your heart and let it **shine**.

Real

Revealing

Epic

Authentic

Lifestyle

Be **real**, be yourself!

Realistic

Realizing

Everything

Acts

Like

Imaginary

Spontaneously

Triggering

Inner

Clarity

Be passionate and **realistic**.

Pure

Positively
Utterly
Ridiculously
Exemplary

Be motivated by **pure** love.

Blameless

Being
Lovingly
Aware,
Mistakes
Educate,
Love
Erases,
Self
Sustains

We are **blameless**—now, let's go and live it!

Confident

Choose

Openly,

Never

Fear,

Ideas

Decide,

Expression

Notifies,

Truth

Let's be **confident** in all we do.

Release

Relax

Enjoying

Life

Especially

After

Stress

Ended

Release old habits.

Truthful

Today
Remember
Unceasingly
Thirst
Honesty,
Fairness,
Unacceptable
Lies

Being **truthful** is at the core of understanding.

Capable

Consistent

Ability

Portrayed

Always

Because

Love

Exists

We are **capable** beyond words.

Delight

Definitely
Enjoying
Life,
Indeed
Grandkids
Heighten
Titter

What a **delight** grandchildren are!

Assured

Actually

Seeing

Self

Unquestionably

Right

Enduring

Discrimination

Be **assured** that life does not wait for anyone.

See

Searching
Everywhere
Everyday

See the beauty within yourself.

Gentle

Gifted

Energy

Nice

Tender

Loving

Easy

Take out your **gentle** spirit and share it.

Comfort

Caring
Offered
Moves
Freeing
Others
Rendering
Thanks

Comfort those who suffer.

Natural

Not
Artificial
True
Untouched
Real
Always
Likable

Natural is how we are when we are
not trying to be normal.

Playful

Performing
Life's
Acts
Yet
Fun
Ultra
Lesson

Live life with a **playful** soul.

Relationship

Realizing

Everyone

Lives

Among

Their

Individual

Opportunity

Notably

Sharing

Helping

Is

Purpose

All **relationships** require effort.

Admirable

A

Dedicated

Mother

Ingeniously

Relishes

Alternatively

Believing

Life

Endures

Our daughter Lindsay inspired this saying –
Sept 2016.

Appealing

Acknowledging

Purposeful

Potential,

Everything

Attracts

Lovingly,

Interesting

New

Goal

Let your senses acquire what is **appealing**
and beautiful.

Enthusiastic

Enjoying

Numerous

Times,

Having

Ultimate

Satisfaction

Inadvertently

Admiring,

Savoring

The

Initial

Choice

Be **enthusiastic** with your choices.

Talented

Totally
Acknowledging
Life's
Endowment,
Naturally
Trained,
Emerging
Display

Bring out your **talented** side.

Strong

Surely
Tuned,
Reaching
Obvious
Nurtured
Growth

Keeping the body healthy keeps the
mind **strong.**

Wonderful

While

Openly

Noticing

Declaring

Excellent

Reaction

Fuels

Unlimited

Lives

How **wonderful** life can be!

Being

Benevolent

Essence

Inner

Natural

Grounding

Let's try **being** who we really are!

Peace

Perception

Essentially

Appeased

Calmness

Exists

Peace be with you.

Heart

Hearing
Echoes
Announcing
Real
Truths

Listen to your **heart**!

Values

Valuable

Attitudes

Lure

Unprecedented

Ethics

Synchronously

Stay true to your **values**.

Chance

Challenge
Helps
Ability,
New
Choice
Exists

Thank God for another **chance** to do our best.

Energy

Every

Needed

Element

Relatively

Growing

You

It takes very little **energy** to be kind.

Life

Learning

Initiating

Free

Expression

Life unfolds as we choose it to.

Stop

Seriously

Time

Out

Please

Stop thinking so much!

Mind

Many
Images
Never-ending
Displays

A positive **mind** produces a positive life.

Body

Building
Of
Dense
Yield

Give your **body** the food and exercise it deserves.

Dream

Desire
Really
Expedites,
Aspiration
Manifests

A **dream** contains all your inner thoughts.

Trust

Tolerating
Relaxing
Understanding
Simple
Truths

Trust your heart!

Sweet

So
Wonderful,
Extremely
Enjoyable
Treasure

Be **sweet**!

Grace

Gifted

Regular

Action

Conveying

Ease

Pay attention and witness the moments of **grace**.

Cheerful

Clearly

Having

Elated

Enthusiasm

Realistically

Fulfilling

Umpteen

Lives

A **cheerful** demeanor is contagious.

*W*ithin

With
Intuition,
Trials
Heartache
Instinct
Nullifies

If we do not go **within**, we go without.

Unloving

Unveiling

Negative

Littleness

Only

Volcanizes

Ideas

Neglecting

Goodness

Never see yourself as **unloving.**

Better

Best
Effort,
Trying
Tediously,
Eventual
Recognition

We are all **better** off having grown
through tough times.

Create

Causing
Reaction,
Every
Action
Thought
Evolves

Every thought, every word, and every
act **creates** our life.

Goodness

Giving

Openly

Offers

Depth,

Neglecting

Ego

Serves

Soul

Recognize your inner **goodness**.

*T*hink

Thoughts
Happen
Instantaneously,
Negotiating
Kick-started

Let's **think** before we speak.

Change

Challenging,

How

Are

New

Goals

Experienced?

Change your attitude, change the results.

Understand

Unique

Nature

Deciphers

Explicitly

Recognizing

Someone's

Truth

And

Not

Disagreeing

Being loving is to **understand**.

Accept

Awarding

Conscious

Compassion

Even

Proceeding

Temptation

Accept what every day has to offer.

Healer

Having
Exemplary
Abilities
Leaving
Everyone
Relaxed

We all have the ability to **heal**.

Together

To
Only
Gather
Enough
Times
Happily
Entertaining
Relatives

Working **together** brings success!

Simplify

Seriously

Ignoring

Materialism

Pro

Living

In

Freedom

Years

Let us **simplify** our lives.

$\mathcal{T}ime$

Taking

Individual

Moments

Earnestly

Time is swift; make the most of it.

Have

Helping
Another
Verifies
Existence

What we **have** must be shared.

Can

Capable

And

Nurturing

Let's do good when we **can**.

$\mathcal{K}$nack

Knowing

Natural

Aptitude

Crazy

Knowledge

We all have a special **knack**.

Mercy

May

Everyone

Rejoice

Constant

Yearning

Show **mercy** to others.

Joy

Just
Opportunity
Yesterday

The **joy** is in living every moment earnestly.

Discover

Digging

Into

Something

Completely

Overwhelming

Verifies

Existing

Realities

Expand your horizons and **discover** your True Self.

Bold

Busting
Open
Levels,
Determined

Let's be **bold** and seek from life
what we really want.

Manifest

Momentarily

Accepting,

Nothing

Impossible,

For

Ever

Stay

Tuned

Manifest your dreams!

Write

With
Real
Intelligence
Tell
Everyone

Write and create yourself.

Drive

Deep
Realization
I
Vehemently
Embark

It only takes a little **drive** to get started.

Compassion

Caring
Offers
Mankind
Power
And
Super
Strength
In
Only
Nanoseconds

Have **compassion** for everyone.

Instinct

Inner

No

Suddenly

Tells

Intuition

Negative

Clear

Truth

Follow your **instinct**!

Mercy

May
Everyone
Really
Carefully
Yield

God's **mercy** never tires.

Decide

Determine
Experience,
Conclude
Irrevocably,
Destiny
Exposed

Decide to live with an open heart.

Joyous

Just

Open

Your

Obnoxious

Unusual

Self

Share your **joyous** Self!

Help

Having
Excellent
Loving
Passion

Help your neighbor.

Worthy

Wielding

Opportunity

Reliable

True

Hardworking

You

We are **worthy** of the perfect experience.

Teacher

Taking

Energy

And

Commitment,

Helping

Educate,

Rewarding

We are our children's **teacher**.

Still

Silent
Till
I
Literally
Listen

Be **still** and listen!

$\mathscr{S}$trength

Standing
Tall,
Really
Energized,
Notably
Geared
Towards
Healthiness

Loving someone gives them **strength**.

Forgiveness

Forget

Offense,

Releasing

Guilt

Internally,

Very

Exuberant

Negating

Experience,

Something

Special

Forgiveness is always possible.

Knowledge

Keep
Needing
Opportunities
Which
Lovingly
Enlighten
Demanding
Growth
Enormously

Knowledge is the wisdom of knowing
that we know.

$\mathcal{P}$ropel

Potential

Rush

Of

Pushing

Encouragement,

Love

Propel your loved ones in the right direction.

Action

A

Conscious

Treatment

Inner

Outer

Narration

Judge not the **actions** of another.

✐Admit

Address
Diligently
Matters
Involving
Truth

Admit to ourselves who you really are.

Death

Departure
Entering
Afterlife
Through
Heaven

Death is not the end.

Patience

Politely

Anticipating

That

Inescapably

Everything

Naturally

Continues

Evolving

Patience and good behavior go hand in hand.

Afraid

Always
Fearing
Really
Allowing
Inner
Discomforts

It is OK to be **afraid**.

Open

Of
Permanent
Exposure
Now

Be **open** to the flow of life, and then the magic happens.

Freedom

Fresh

Relaxing

Exciting

Enjoying

Diverse

Outdoor

Moments

Seek courage, and we will find **freedom**.

First

Figuring
Initially,
Rightfully
Self
Trusts

First things first!

Desire

Deeply
Entertaining
Serious
Ideas
Rendering
Enthusiasm

The **desire** to love should exceed
the desire to be loved.

Service

Simple
Encouragement
Reaches
Via
Implementing
Comfortable
Effort

Be of **service** to others and your true Self appears.

Tolerant

Totally

Open

Letting

Excessive

Rebellious

Annoying

Nonsense

Tease

To be **tolerant** is to not judge.

Safe

Sweet
Angel
Friends
Everywhere

Feeling **safe** is a choice.

*H*appy

Had
A
Pretty
Perfect
Yesterday

Happy lies within your thoughts.

Affirmation

Allowing

Friendly

Frequent

Intentions

Repeatedly

Maintaining

A

Truth

In

Oneself

Naturally

Try a positive **affirmation** every day.

Goal

Getting

Objectives

All

Lineal

Our life's main **goal** is to nurture a positive Self.

Self

Solely
Enriching
Life's
Features

Our main focus is loving **Self**.

Worry

Wondering

Often

Restless

Ruffled

You

Worry never robs tomorrow of its sorrow;
it only saps today of its strength.

Integrity

Important
Never
To
Erupt,
Guided
Rationally
In
Thoughtful
Yore

May our children equate **integrity** with us.

Where

Which
Has
Ended,
Review,
Engage

It is not **where** we are; it is where we are headed.

Scary

Something
Central
Abandons
Real
You

It is only **scary** if we want it to be.

Opinion

Of
Personal
Importance
Not
Inviting
Others'
Notions

Our **opinions** do count.

Conquers

Control
One's
Natural
Quick
Urge
Ending
Radical
Sabotage

Loving others conquers our love for Self!

Adapt

Amazing
Dexterity
Applied
Per
Tribulation

To **adapt** is to be open to the amazing part of you.

ℒrocrastinate

Postponing
Relevant
Opportunity
Criticizing
Realistic
Abilities
Some
Tension
Involved
Not
Able
To
Evolve

To **procrastinate** is to pedal backwards.

Ridiculous

Rendering

Idiotic

Dumb

Ideas

Creating

Useless

Life

Opportunities

Under

Stress

To take anything personally or to assume anything is **ridiculous**.

Deeper

Dampen
Egotistic
Energy
Pursuing
Ethereal
Reasons

Deeper thoughts bring better choices.

Trust

To
Rely
Upon,
Seriously
Thankful

Trust those we love!

Wise

Who
Instinctually
Sees
Exactness

Let's be **wise** in our choices.

Decide

Drama
Ensues,
Concluding
Intervenes,
Determining
Eventually

We won't let others **decide** for us.

Life

Living
Intuitively
Figuratively
Emotionally

Life is worth living!

Doing

Decidely
Operating,
Initiating
Natural
Giving

We will keep **doing** what we're doing
if it feels right.

Victim

Varying
Ideas
Compounded
Torment
Instilling
Misery

Don't be a **victim**!

Procrastinate

Postponing
Reveals
Outward
Confusion,
Reviewing
And
Searching
Travels
Inward,
Not
Acting
Terminates
Execution

We no longer **procrastinate** when we welcome the daily challenges.

Reason

Reference
Existing
Attitude
Summon
Opinion
Necessary

There is a **reason** for everything.

Nothing

Noting
Often
That
Here
Is
Never-ending
Greatness

Nothing can stop our dreams.

Soul

Settled

Omnisciently

Upon

Love

Our **souls** are connected as one.

Energy

Everything
Naturally
Emanates
Revealing
Grand
Yield

The **energy** to heal can be spoken.

Work

Wanting
One's
Responsibilities
Known

Hard **work** never killed anyone.

Master

Meticulously

Adept,

Sincerely

Truthful,

Evermore

Realistic

Let's be the **master** of our own destiny.

Concern

Constant

Obsessing,

Never

Calm,

Everything

Relevant

Now

Only be **concerned** with yourself.

Required

Rules

Expectations

Qualifying,

Umpteen

Imaginary

Reasons,

Everyone

Dreams

Nothing is **required** from anyone.

Does

Diligently
Operates
Effectively
Succeeding

Healing **does** come in many different forms.

Perfect

Pretty

Effortlessly

Respecting

Feverishly

Exact

Communication

Task

The **perfect** gift is to give without thought of reward.

Guard

Genuinely
Unbelievably
Afraid
Reacts
Dangerously

Let's never **guard** ourselves against love.

Always

Again
Life
Will
Acknowledge
Your
Strengths

Always love, **always** share, and **always** believe.

Aim

Aware

Invent

Manifest

Aim for the stars!

Envious

Eagerly

Noticing,

Vigilant

In

Others

Unimportant

Status

To be **envious** is to doubt Self.

Confirm

Cause
Of
Noting
For
It
Really
Matters

We **confirm** that we believe in Self.

Spirit

Simply

Put

It

Really

Is

Truth

Let your **Spirit** shine!

Fear

Foreign
Energy
Abolished
Rational

Never **fear** the worst.

Ideas

Implementing

Descriptive

Energy

And

Symbolizing

Ideas are our inner creations.

Condemn

Criticizing
Offends,
Never
Displaying
Enough
Motherly
Notions

Let's never **condemn** what we
do not understand.

Resist

Restrain

Existing

Situations

Inadvertently

Speeds

Tension

We **resist** what we fear.

Disease

Decisions
Import
Suffering,
Enjoyment
Annihilated,
Serenity
Eliminated

When **disease** knocks on your door, don't invite it in.

New

Never
Experienced
Within

Out with the old, in with the **new**.

Hurting

Helpless,
Unintentional
Rejection
Traumatized
Individual
Needing
Guidance

Love those who are **hurting**.

Create

Conveying

Real

Energy

And

Transmitting

Ethereally

When we **create**, we are amazed.

Purpose

Providing
Us
Reason
Particularly
Once
Someone
Evolves

Life's **purpose** is to know Self.

Tools

Things
Occurring
Opening
Love
Simultaneously

Let's use the **tools** God has given us.

Great

Generous
Real
Empathetic
Actions
Transform

Let's be as **great** as we can be.

Obedience

Openly
Blocking
Every
Deep
Instinct
Endowed
Naturally
Creating
Emotion

When we are fair and honest,
obedience is not necessary.

Minor

Most
Inferior
Noxious
Opportunity
Revealed

Don't major in **minor** things.

Courage

Conscious

Open

Understanding,

Real

Adventuresome

Gutsy

Experience

Courage is fear that has said its prayers.

Self

Singularly
Experiencing
Life's
Fullness

Be kind to **Self**!

Optimism

Open
Pensive
Thought
Involving
Major
Indisputable
Sound
Moments

Optimism holds the door open
to a promising tomorrow.

Beauty

Bustling
Energy,
Adorable,
Undisturbed,
Tension
Yielded

Think of all the **beauty** that surrounds us.

Dirt

Damage

Imposed

Ruined

Truth

Someone else's **dirt** has nothing to do with us.

Another

Acknowledge

Noble

Outstanding

Talented

Human

Equal

Rights

What we do for **another**, we do for Self.

Waste

Won't
Appreciate
Something,
Throwing
Elsewhere

Never **waste** anything.

Menial

Matter
Expressing
Nonsense
Insignificant
Average
Lowly

A **menial** attitude brings no success.

Good

Great
Opportunity
Obviously
Disguised

Every day may not be **good**, but there's good in every day.

Respond

Readily
Expressing,
Same
Perception
Obtained
Nearly
Duplicating

Life is not happening to us,
life is **respond**ing to us.

Decide

Determine
Essentially,
Concluding
Immediately,
Definite
Ending

We need to **decide** now how we
are going to live.

Believe

Because

Engaging

Love

Ignites

Essential

Valued

Emotions

Believe in yourself!

Impossible

I
May
Pretend
Opposition
Surrounds,
Somehow
Ignorance
Belittles
Licensing
Ego

Nothing is **impossible**—the word itself
says, "I'm possible!"

$\mathcal{T}$ime

Truth
Is,
Minutes
Expire

Take **time** to love!

$\mathcal{P}$roblem

Perceived

Real

Obstacle

Brings

Lesson

Endogenously

Masked

With every **problem** a gift is given.

Empower

Emotional

Means,

Positive

Opinion

Will

Ethereally

Release

Each time we make the choice to listen to our gut and do right, we **empower** ourselves.

Creator

Continue

Realizing

Effort

And

Time

Offer

Reward

We are the **creators** creating our realities.

Coincidence

Clever

Opportunities

Interfere

Notwithstanding

Confrontation

Indirectly

Deciding,

Eventually

Negotiating

Certain

Events

Is it really a **coincidence** or part
of God's master plan?

Escape

Exit
Something
Catastrophic,
Attempt
Possible
End

We need to **escape** from the prison
of our minds.

Afraid

Apprehensive

For

Right

Ahead

Indicates

Danger

Don't be **afraid** to start living.

Pardon

Politely

Acknowledge,

Releasing

Damaging

Ominous

Notions

Pardon yourself.

Fear

Feeling

Evermore

Afraid

Recognized

Feel the **fear** and move on.

Light

Let
It
Glow
Healing
Touch

Be a **light** in someone's life.

Surrender

Serious

Understanding

Really

Recognizes

Easing

Nonsense

Drama

Eliminating

Rhetoric

Surrender to the moment,
and life will unfold magically.

Now

New
Opportunity
Waiting

The perfect time to start anew is **Now**!

Bravo

Because
Respecting
Another
Validates
Ovation

Bravo to you who disengages the guilt,
the fear, the old habits, and the need
for love to realize who you really are.

ℒearn

Live
Even
After
Rearing
Negativity

Learn from your mistakes!

Heavenly

Having
Excellent
Attributes,
Very
Exquisite,
Naturally
Lifting
You

Watch a **heavenly** sunset.

Positive

Possessing

Open

Sentiment,

Innately

Trusting

In

Various

Expressions

Positive thinking knows that good exists.

Me

Myself
Exactly

Sometimes I pretend to be normal.
It gets boring, so I go back to being **me**.

Virtue

Vibrant
In
Righteous
Truthful
Upstanding
Ethics

Virtue blesses us with peace.

Can't

Confronting
Again
Negative
Tales

Never say, "I **can't**".

More

Moving
Openly
Receiving
Eternally

Talk less, say **more**!

Prayer

Politely

Requesting

Assistance

Yielding

Encouragement

Relaxation

Prayer is life's secret cure.

Rising

Redoing

Inspires

Satisfaction,

Ignoring

Negative

Guilt

Rising above all difficulties.

Room

Recognizing
Openness
Occurs
Masterfully

Where there is **room** in the heart,
there is always **room** in the house.

Dishonest

Disrespecting

Inner

Soul

However

Oblivious,

Needlessly

Expressing

Self-centered

Truth

A **dishonest** act unearths troubles
further down the road.

Bend

Be
Expansive
Not
Determined

Better **bend** than break.

Peaceful

Proof

Exists,

Acting

Calm

Exalts

Fulfilling

Unsettled

Lives

Peaceful is one who loves without expectation.

Wise

What
Insightful
Sound
Expression

Be **wise** in your travels.

Thoughts

Those
Heartfelt
Open
Understandings
Gathered
Having
To
Scrutinize

Take time to stop and capture your **thoughts**.

Stepping

Simple

Travel

Enabled

Presenting

Possibilities

In

Numerous

Genres

There is power in **stepping** beyond your comfort zone.

Concepts

Concrete

Opinions

Need

Communicating

Exposing

Practical

Teachings

Simultaneously

Teach your children wholesome **concepts** such as honesty, compassion, and responsibility.

Plan

Particularly

Limiting

Anything

Natural

We never look back unless we **plan** to go that way.

Creativity

Concepts

Realized,

Excellent

Abilities

That

Instinctively

Visualize

Inviting

True

Yield

Creativity is maximized when we are living in the moment.

Reflection

Reaction

Everyone

Feels

Leaves

Energy

Communicating,

Tremendous

Impression

Often

Noticed

Our outlook on life is a direct **reflection** of how much we like ourselves.

Transform

To
Realize
Altering
Naturally
Simply
Flips
Onto
Renewal
Mode

Love can **transform** your life!

*O*pen

Obliterating
Preexisting
Entering
New

Open your mind before your mouth.

Alone

Accept

Lifelong

Omission

Never

Ends

Be **alone**, be brave, discover self,
no interruptions.

Care

Continued
Affection
Reaching
Everyone

To **care** for another brings courage.

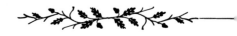

Fair

Freely
Accepting
Individual
Responses

Be **fair**!

Bad

Better
Adjust
Demeanor

There is always something good that comes out of something **bad**.

Never

Not
Ever
Vacating,
Evermore
Rigid

Never stop loving!

Good

Gentle

Optimistic

Often

Desirable

Always try to have **good** thoughts.

Be

Better
Enjoy

Let us **be** the people we truly want to be.

Important

Involves

Main

Priorities

Overriding

Ridiculous

Temptations

Altering

Nurturing

Times

Make your family your most **important** focus.

Simplicity

Streamlining

Intention

Means

Putting

Little

Interesting

Choices

In

Top

Yield

To give your children joy,
teach them **simplicity**.

Sorry

Sincerely
Openly
Responding
Regretfully
Yahweh

Being **sorry** helps the heart grow.

Courage

Compliment

Oneself

Understanding

Respect

Affection

Gratitude

Everyday

Inspire **courage** within every day.

Mistake

Mainly
Insufficient
Self confidence
That
Annuls
Knowing
Exactly

Never fear that you will make a **mistake**.

Conflict

Control

Only

Neglects

Faith

Leading

Into

Confusing

Thoughts

Avoid **conflict**!

Applause

Acknowledging
Politely
Particular
Life
Accomplishments,
Understanding
Something
Exceptional

Applaud yourself; **applause** from others
does not matter.

Capable

Constantly

Assuming

Positive

Ability

Being

Little

Effort

We are **capable** of love.

Bring

Bestow

Real

Ideas

Naturally

Gifted

Bring forth all your talents.

Serve

Solemnly

Effortlessly

Return

Valued

Effort

Serve all mankind!

Pain

Particularly
Annoying
Invested
Notions

Focusing on **pain** increases its depth.

Resent

Rational
Exempt,
Sabotaging
Everything,
Negative
Terms

To **resent** has a boomerang effect.

Tears

This
Expresses
Authentic
Reactive
Sadness

Tears should be saved for those
who won't make us cry.

Confused

Concluding

Obvious

Negative

Frustration

Undergoing

Such

Entangled

Drama

Never **confuse** your mind with your emotions.

$\mathcal{H}$appy

Honest

Apparent

Peaceful

Perky

You

Happy times are undervalued.

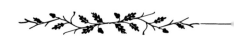

Known

Kindly

Noting

Obtaining

Wisdom

Naturally

We have all **known** right from wrong.

Reverence

Respect

Everyone

Value

Everything

Realizing

Empathy

Naturally

Concedes

Enjoyment

To offer **reverence** to all mankind
is to love God.

Forgive

Fully

Openly

Release

Guilt

Initiating

Valuable

Exercise

Forgive yourself!

Laugh

Live
Audibly
Understand
Genuine
Happiness

Laughter is freedom from your own inner critic.

Dance

Delightful

Act

Naturally

Consuming

Energy

When we **dance**, our soul is speaking.

Smile

Single
Moment
Initiates
Loving
Energy

Let's **smile** when life throws us a hard ball.

*M*oment

Minute

Opportunities

Magically

Eliminated

Numerous

Times

Live in the **moment**!

Most

Mastering
Overall
Special
Times

The happiest people make the
most of everything.

Bless

Beneficial

Leaving

Everyone

Sensing

Secure

Loving words send **blessings**.

$\mathcal{K}$ind

Knowing

Inspiration

Never

Dies

To be **kind** costs nothing.

*T*ime

Thousand
Individual
Moments
Erased

Don't waste **time**.

See

Suddenly
Experience
Excitement

We can **see** the light at the end of the tunnel.

Joyful

Just

Openly

Yearning

Faith

Understanding

Love

Joy is a comfortable state beyond happiness.

Guilt

Gradually
Unveiling
Internally
Life's
Troubles

Ditch the **guilt**!

ℐAct

Always
Confirming
Talent

Every **act** defines Self.

Decide

Displaying
Eagerness
Commands
Immediate
Definite
End

Let's take time every day to remind
ourselves of what we **decided** yesterday.

Serenity

Silence

Enables

Realizing

Emptiness

Naturally

Illuminates

Tremendous

Yield

God grant me the **serenity** to accept
my True Self.

Kindness

Knowing

Invaluable

Niceness

Delivers

Never

Even

Speculating

Sometimes

Kindness is the creator of love and confidence.

Charity

Conveying

Honest

Affectionate

Real

Interpersonal

Transparent

You

Charity is a form of right-mindedness.

Emotions

Energy

Moving

Only

To

Ignite

Optimum

Natural

Sensitivity

Emotions are an act of will.

Restores

Rebuilding

Exercise

Seems

Troublesome

Often

Realizing

Exemplary

Symptoms

Pay attention to your body
and **restore** its good health.

Master

Most
Astounding
Soul
Touching
Expertise
Revealed

To **master** your world is to allow life to unfold naturally.

Align

Aftermath

Locates

Immense

Gratitude

Naturally

The healthy body **aligns** with a healthy mind.

Power

Pure
Omnipotent
Wonderful
Energy
Raging

We have the **power** to heal ourselves.

Beauty

Because
Everything
Acts
Unique
To
You

Look outside and witness the **beauty** in nature.

Give

Graciously
Invest,
Valuable
Exercise

Give from your heart!

Willingness

With
Inner
Love
Letting
Intuition
Naturally
Grasp
Now
Enthusiastically
Submitting
Self

Our appreciation for life's abundance grants us the **willingness** to share our abundance.

Happiness

Heartfelt

Attitude

Projected

Positively

Illuminates

Natural

Energy

Seeking

Sunshine

Happiness is waiting for everyone.

Small

Simply

Making

Affordable

Life

Lessons

Every **small** act of kindness is a gift to someone.

Freedom

Finding

Real

Enjoyment,

Emotions

Dissolved

Objective

Mind

Give yourself the **freedom** to love openly.

Yourself

You

Opening

Up

Releasing

Soul

Expressive

Love

First

As you see another, you will see **yourself**.

Keep

Kindly
Embracing
Everything
Positive

In order to **keep** it, we must give it.

Withdraw

With
Immediate
Thought
Help
Demonstrate
Real
Authentic
Wisdom

Withdraw from all egotistical thoughts.

Deny

Demonstrating

Egotistical

Neglectful

Yearning

To **deny** another, we will only be denying Self.

Teach

To
Enlighten
Another
Communicates
Happiness

Teach your children love so that they know who they really are.

Challenge

Confidence

Helps

Alleviate

Letting

Life's

Ego

Nonsense

Graciously

Evaporate

Life will **challenge** us to seek perfection.

$\mathscr{S}$weet

Succulent

Wave

Excreting

Exciting

Taste

Enjoy life's **sweet**ness.

Fear

Forgetting
Expecting
Allowing
Regretting

Living in **fear** is not living.

News

North

East

West

South

This was **news** to me.

Decide

Distinguish

Exact

Concrete

Ideas

Denoting

Existence

Decide to live in, with, and around Love.

Appreciate

Acknowledge

Precious

Potential

Really

Exists,

Cherishing

Individuals

Always

Transforms

Everyone

Fear makes **appreciation** impossible.

Emotions

Every

Minute

Occurring

Thoughts

Ignite

Obtaining

New

Symptoms

Control your **emotions**!

Within

Wearing
It,
The
Human
Intuitive
Nature

Look **within;** we have all the answers.

Co-creator

Cooperate
Openly,
Complimenting
Real
Exceptional
Authentic
Traits
Others
Release

We are **co-creators**!

$\mathscr{A}$ttack

Alien

Twisted

Thought

Always

Countermands

Knowledge

To **attack** anyone is to attack Self.

Totality

Today
One
Thought
Aspiring
Love,
Inspiring
Togetherness
Yet

Understand totally by understanding **totality**.

Gift

Giving

It

First

Thought

God has **gift**ed each and everyone.

You

Yielding
Oneself's
Understanding

You decide your destiny!

Hell

Horribly
Explained
Life
Lesson

We may feel we are living a life of **hell,**
but we will never go to hell.

Effect

Evidently
Favorable/
Faux pas,
Exact
Concluding
Theme

We do feel the **effect**s of negative attitudes.

Cause

Can
Anyone
Understand
Simple
Effect

Only we can **cause** our unhappiness.

$\mathcal{P}$roject

Personally

Reflecting

Outstanding

Justifiable

Earnest

Conclusive

Traits

We **project** our belief in Self.

Serve

Simply

Extend

Respect

Versus

Evil

To attack another will not **serve** us well.

$\mathcal{D}o$

Demonstrate
Openly

We listen, we learn but the real magic
is in the **do**ing.

Darken

Discovering

Absolute

Rhetoric

Knows

Everlasting

Nothing

To be untrue to self is to **darken** our path.

Deceive

Decide
Every
Circumstance,
Egoism
Involved,
Validates
Error

To **deceive** ourselves is to believe
in our false Selves.

Unconditional

Under
Normal
Circumstances
Offer
New
Decision
Instituting
Total
Immediate
Open
Nonjudgmentally
Acknowledging
Love

Help to instill in another their self-worth
by loving them **unconditional**ly.

Before

By
Envisioning
Fairness
Outstanding
Reaction
Ensues

Let's stop and think **before** we judge.

Offer

Openly
Freeing
Favorable
Expression
Rendered

Offer only love for that is what we are.

Decision

Deeply
Eagerly
Committing,
Intuitively
Seeking
Immediately
One's
Need

Make the **decision** to be positive!

Perceive

Peacefully

Extricating

Reasonable

Conclusions

Eventually

Invites

Valuable

Enjoyment

Perceive another always as innocent.

Change

Consistently

Honoring

A

New

Growing

Experience

Changing your thoughts changes your life.

Feed

Fantastic
Ethereal
Energy
Distributed

Spending time in nature **feed**s the soul.

Heal

Heaven
Encourages
Awakening
Love

Healing your mind heals the body.

Depression

Dismayed

Entirely

Perhaps

Reduced

Energy

Symptoms

Somewhat

Illustrating

Outstanding

Negativity

Depression is to believe that we are lacking.
Be grateful and loving.

Distract

Decide

Investing

Some

Time

Relaxing

Acquiring

Conscious

Thoughts

Distracting ourselves with positive ideas
brings strength.

Quiet

Quintessential

Undisturbed

Iridescent

Energy

Trapped

Sit in the **quiet** stillness of your mind.

Way

Whatever's
Appealing
Yin/yang

Our hearts show us the right **way;**
we just have to stop and listen.

Present

Perfectly

Relaxing

Enjoying

Simple

Events

Notably

Today

Live in the **present** moment!

Different

Diverting

In

Forward

Fashion

Each

Rendering

Exclusive

Natural

Trials

A **different** path must be walked by everyone.

Difficulty

Dilemma

Involving

Frustration

Feels

Immensely

Complicated

Until

Life

Teaches

You

We see **difficulty;** God sees potential.

Destructive

Damaging

Emotional

Suicide

Transforms

Reality

Unconsciously

Complicating

Truth

Ignoring

Valuable

Existence

Why do we choose to be self-**destructive**?

Destiny

Distant

Expectations

Somehow

Turn

Into

Natural

Yield

Dream of a beautiful **destiny**!

Let Go

Leave
Everything
Transpire

Generous
Offering

Let go of all the pain!

Need

Negative

Existence

Extreme

Dependence

All we **need** is love!

Evolution

Every
Version
Of
Life
Unravels
Times
Interesting
Or
Numbing

We must **evolve** into who we really are.

Eternal

Everlasting,

Time

Erased,

Roots

Never-ending

Anima

Lasting

Your soul is **eternal**.

Actions

Admitting

Consciously

To

Initiate

Offers

Never-ending

Solace

Our **actions** demonstrate who we believe we are.

Escape

Eventually
Sidestepping
Confidently
Allowing
Personal
Extrication

Escape the negativity.

$\mathcal{T}$hrough

To
Heal
Realize
Opportunity
Ultimately
Greets
Hell

What we must go **through** …..!

*N*one

No
One
Needs
Evil

Do wrong to **none**.

𝒯 hought

To

Hover

Opinions

Un-expectantly

Getting

Haphazard

Truth

Keep your **thought**s positive!

Absence

Avoiding

Bitter

Sarcastic

Emotions,

Not

Currently

Existing

An **absence** of judgment opens one up to love.

$\mathcal{S}$ilence

Stillness

Illustrates

Loving

Energy

Noting

Chaotic

Extinction

Welcome the **silence**!

Rainbow

Rays
Accentuating
Illustrious
Natural
Beauty,
Opulent
Watercolors

A **rainbow** shines hope in our lives.

Solve

Solutions
Overcoming
Life's
Vexation
Explained

To **solve** a problem is to forgive and forget.

*L*ove

Lifts

Open

Values

Everything

Love is the answer!

*E*go

Evil
Guidance
Oppresses

Avoid being **ego**-driven.

ℐAbundance

Accepting

Believing

Understanding

Not

Denying

All

Numerous

Capabilities

Everyday

When we acknowledge the **abundance**
in our lives, we are thankful.

Steer

Steadily

Try

Encouraging

Ethic

Righteousness

Steer your life in the right direction.

$\mathcal{H}$elp

Have

Enough

Love

Potential

Always **help** another without question.

Best

Bestowing
Energy
Sweat
Tears

We always do our **best**!

Wrong

Worldly
Reality
Only
Negates
Growth

It is not right or **wrong;** it is an experience.

Shackled

Something
Horrible
Abound
Constantly
Killing
Life,
Ego
Demands

We are slaves **shackled** not by iron but by debt.

Achieve

And
Concluding
Hope
I
Enlightened
Various
Entities

I hope I **achieve**d my goal of helping
others believe that they are perfect in
their own uniqueness.

About the Author

Michelle Sierens is an avid reader and writer. She is a wife, mother and grand-mother who adores her family. She loves the early morning and finds inspiration in the forest around her home in Northern Alberta where she lives with her husband. This is her first book.

Author picture by www.lovelynestphotography.com

Word List

CPSIA information can be obtained
at www.ICGtesting.com
Printed in the USA
LVOW11s0125280418
575223LV00001B/48/P